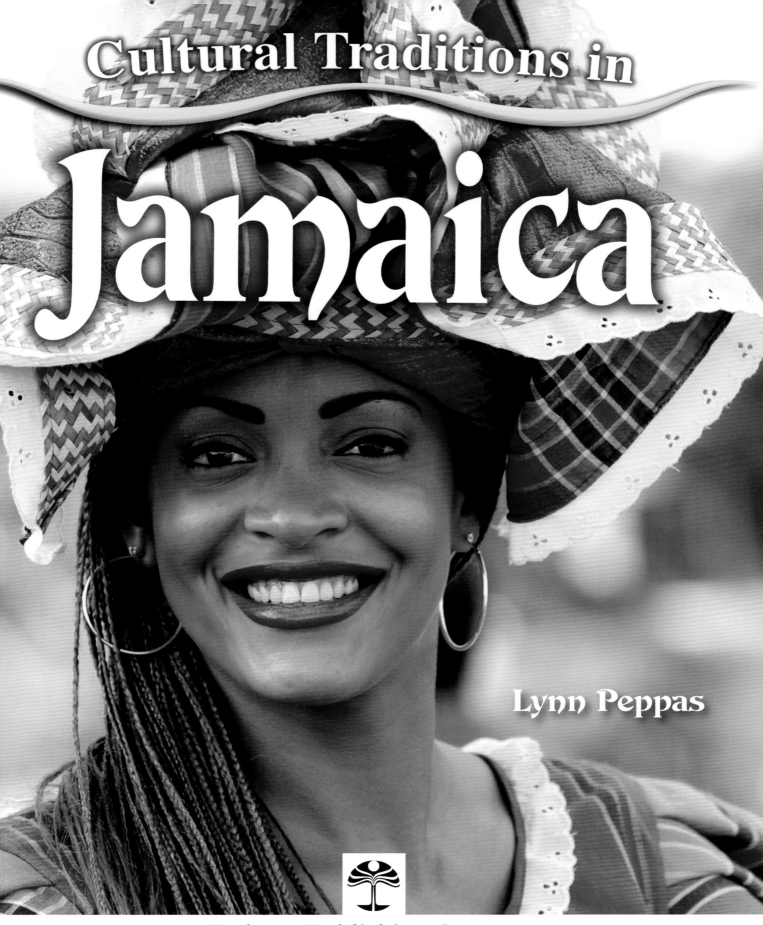

Cultural Traditions in Jamaica

Jamaica

Lynn Peppas

Crabtree Publishing Company

www.crabtreebooks.com

Crabtree Publishing Company

www.crabtreebooks.com

Author: Lynn Peppas
Publishing plan research and development:
  Reagan Miller
Editors: Rebecca Sjonger, Kathy Middleton
Proofreader and indexer: Wendy Scavuzzo
Design: Tammy McGarr
Photo research: Tammy McGarr, Crystal Sikkens
Production coordinator and prepress technician:
  Tammy McGarr
Print coordinator: Margaret Amy Salter

Cover: A kite with the Jamaican flag (top); Tropical beach with passenger boats (background); Tambour drum (bottom right); Dancer in colorful clothes (right); Tending a young avocado plant (bottom middle); A rasta in traditional clothes (left); Jerk chicken (top dish); Callaloo with fried dumplings and plantains (middle dish); Ackee and fish (bottom dish)

Title page: Woman wearing Jamaican national costume for cultural display at Governor General's Residence, Kings House, Kingston, Jamaica:

Photographs:
Alamy: ©JTB MEDIA CREATION, Inc.: pg29
AP Images: Collin Reid: pg 24, p 25 (right), p27
Archivefarms: p22
Bridgeman Images: Johnston, Harry Hamilton (1858-1927) / ©Royal Geographical Society: p10
Corbis: ©Bojan Brecelj: p7; ©Tony Arruza: p11; ©Jeff Albertson: p14; ©Doug Pearson/JAI: p18
Getty Images: Tim Graham: p5 (top); Shelby Soblick: p13; Geography Photos: pg 17; Keystone-France: p26;
iStock: peeterv: cover: (top), p12 (bottom); p19 (bottom right)
Le Antonios Foundation: p21 (top & middle left)
Ray Chen: p31
Shutterstock: ©Andrew Park: cover (middle right); ©John de la Bastide: p16; cover (background, middle and bottom left, bottom middle and right), pp4 (map), 4-5 (background), 25 (flag) 28
Superstock: Tim Graham / Robert Harding Picture Library: title page; Eye Ubiquitous: p15; Alvaro Leiva / age footstock: pg 15 (inset)
Thinkstock: pp6, 21 (bottom left), 23
Wikimedia Commons: creative commons: p12 (inset); creative commons: p19 (top left); creative commons: p20

Illustration:
Ben Hodson: p30

Library and Archives Canada Cataloguing in Publication

Peppas, Lynn, author
          Cultural traditions in Jamaica / Lynn Peppas.

(Cultural traditions in my world)
Includes index.
Issued in print and electronic formats.
ISBN 978-0-7787-8062-5 (bound).--ISBN 978-0-7787-8067-0 (pbk.).--
ISBN 978-1-4271-9960-7 (pdf).--ISBN 978-1-4271-9955-3 (html)

          1. Holidays--Jamaica--Juvenile literature. 2. Festivals--Jamaica--
Juvenile literature. 3. Jamaica--Social life and customs--Juvenile
literature. I. Title. II. Series: Cultural traditions in my world

GT4827.A2P46 2015   j394.2697292   C2014-907789-0
                                                                        C2014-907790-4

Library of Congress Cataloging-in-Publication Data

Peppas, Lynn.
  Cultural traditions in Jamaica / Lynn Peppas.
      pages cm. -- (Cultural traditions in my world)
  Includes index.
  ISBN 978-0-7787-8062-5 (reinforced library binding) --
ISBN 978-0-7787-8067-0 (pbk.) -- ISBN 978-1-4271-9960-7 (electronic pdf) --
ISBN 978-1-4271-9955-3 (electronic html)
  1. Holidays--Jamaica--Juvenile literature. 2. Jamaica--Social life and customs--
Juvenile literature. I. Title.

GT4827.A2B37 2015
394.26097292--dc23

                                                      2014045062

Crabtree Publishing Company

www.crabtreebooks.com   1-800-387-7650

Printed in Canada/042015/EF20150224

Published in Canada
Crabtree Publishing
616 Welland Ave.
St. Catharines, ON
L2M 5V6

Published in the United States
Crabtree Publishing
PMB 59051
350 Fifth Avenue, 59th Floor
New York, New York 10118

Published in the United Kingdom
Crabtree Publishing
Maritime House
Basin Road North, Hove
BN41 1WR

Published in Australia
Crabtree Publishing
3 Charles Street
Coburg North
VIC 3058

Contents

Welcome to Jamaica

Jamaica is an island country in the Caribbean Sea. The Jamaican people are descendants of a number of different groups. Hundreds of years ago, African people were brought to Jamaica to work as slaves. After slavery was **abolished**, Jewish, Chinese, and East Indian immigrants came to work on Jamaica's large farms called **plantations**. Most Jamaicans speak English. Many also speak a language called Jamaican Creole, or *patois*, which is a mix of English, Spanish, and African words.

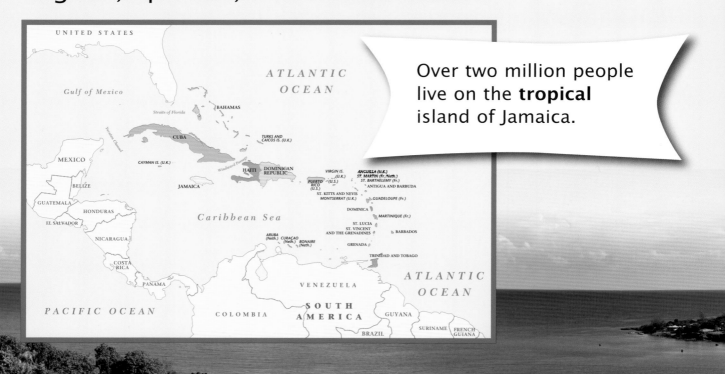

Over two million people live on the **tropical** island of Jamaica.

Jamaica is known worldwide for its music, which includes reggae, folk, and mento. Dancing is also a big part of Jamaican celebrations!

Holidays and festivals in Jamaica are a colorful mix of religious, cultural, and government celebrations. Many holidays are based on the **Christian** religion. A small religion called Rastafari has its roots in Jamaica, but is well known around the world. Rastafarians worship an African king who died in 1975 as their spiritual leader.

Family Celebrations

Wedding celebrations in Jamaica start long before the ceremony. Friends of the couple send gifts of fruit or meat for the wedding dinner before the big day. The bride and groom host an all-night party the night before their wedding. The feasting continues the next day after the ceremony. Curried goat or chicken is usually served. Curry is a spice that immigrants from India brought to Jamaica. Wedding cakes are made with dried fruits and soaked in rum.

Did You Know?
An old wedding custom in Jamaica was for the bride to parade through her town before she was married. Friends and neighbors would shout out comments on how she looked!

Jamaican weddings today are a lot like North American weddings.

When someone dies, people sit up all night playing a game called dominoes, singing songs, and drinking tea, coffee, and rum.

Many traditions from Africa are still practiced in Jamaica. Nine Night is a celebration of a person who has died. It takes place nine days after death. The African slaves believed it took a person's spirit nine days to travel back to Africa after death. If they did not pay enough attention to the spirit, it might cause trouble for the family. Songs are sung to say goodbye, and the dead person's mattress is turned over so the spirit won't stay in the home.

Happy New Year!

On January 1, Jamaicans celebrate the New Year with fireworks and lots of noise from church bells and party horns. Long ago, Jamaicans thought that loud noises scared evil spirits away. Today, people clean and decorate their homes to begin the New Year with a fresh start. Many Jamaicans believe that whatever you do on the first day of a New Year will determine your luck for the rest of the year!

Did You Know? A traditional New Year food for Jamaicans is a soup called Mannish Water. The soup's broth is prepared by boiling the head of a goat.

After watching the lion dance on Chinese New Year, people may enjoy a Chinese stir fry with Jamaican **jerk** chicken.

Chinese Jamaicans celebrate New Year's Day on the first full moon of the **lunar calendar**. That means it is usually on a different day each year, either in late January or early to mid-February. Partygoers are treated to the traditional Chinese lion or dragon dance and enjoy unique dishes that mix Chinese and Jamaican recipes. Fireworks—part of many Jamaican celebrations—were first brought

Cudjoe Day

Some Jamaicans celebrate Cudjoe Day on January 6. This day marks the signing of a peace treaty between the British and a group of escaped slaves. Led by a famous leader named Captain Cudjoe, the group of runaway slaves was called the Maroons. Captain Cudjoe led the fight for the freedom of the Maroons about 400 years ago.

The Maroons escaped and hid in the remote hills of Jamaica, where they lived as free people.

Drumming and singing are all part of the Cudjoe Day celebrations.

Cudjoe Day is celebrated high up in the hills of Jamaica in the town of Accompong. Many people of Maroon **ancestry** still live in the town. During the annual Cudjoe Day festival, Jamaicans and tourists march together to a *Kindah*, or "one family," tree to eat at a feast, listen to music and **folktales**, and dance. The festival begins with the blowing of the Maroon *abeng* war horn. The horn is made from a cow's horn. It was used by the Maroons to communicate during their struggle for freedom.

Musical Salutes

A music-loving nation, Jamaica is famous throughout the world as the birthplace of **reggae** music. Rebel Salute is Jamaica's largest reggae and **dancehall** music festival. It is held every year on the Friday and Saturday closest to January 15—the birthday of Jamaican musician Tony Rebel, who organized the first festival.

Tony Rebel is a follower of the Rastafari religion. Rastafarians do not eat meat or drink alcohol.

Did You Know?
The Rebel Salute music festival offers **vegetarian** dishes of traditional Jamaican foods. No meat or **alcohol** is sold inside the event.

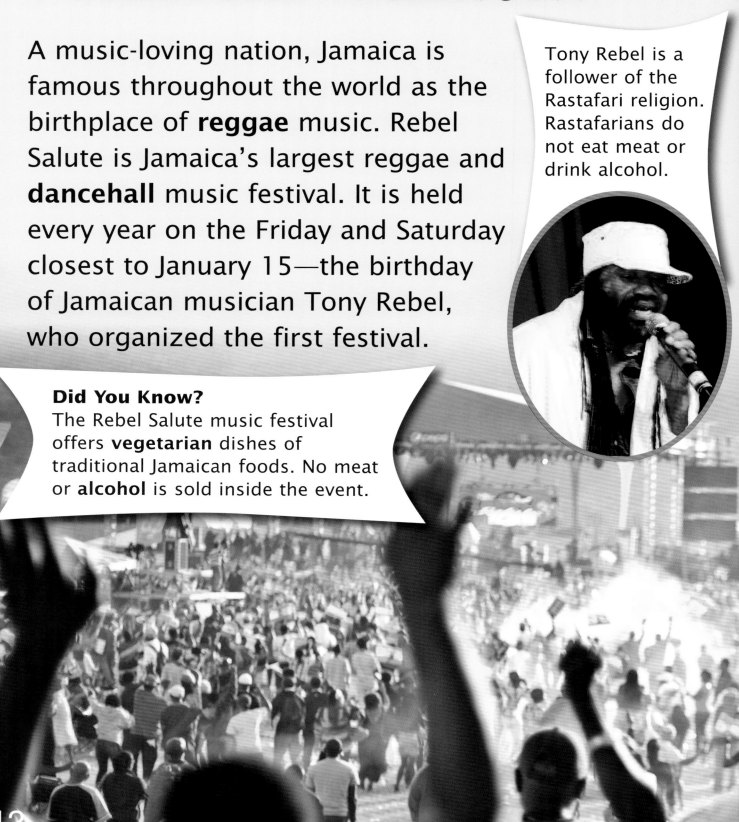

The Rebel Salute festival features roots reggae musicians. Roots reggae is a type of music with **lyrics** about everyday life and **spirituality**. Families, including children, attend this very positive festival. It celebrates Jamaica's unique culture and tries to promote and preserve reggae music.

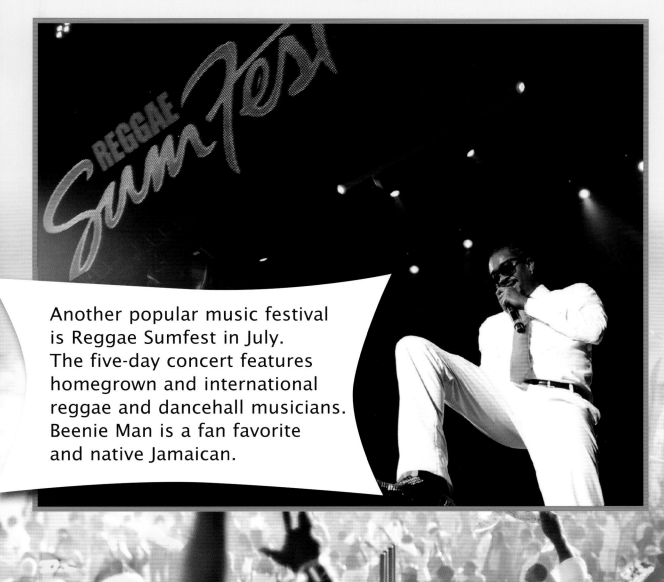

Another popular music festival is Reggae Sumfest in July. The five-day concert features homegrown and international reggae and dancehall musicians. Beenie Man is a fan favorite and native Jamaican.

Bob Marley Day

Bob Marley is Jamaica's most famous reggae musician. He made reggae music popular outside of Jamaica more than any other musician had before him. Jamaicans are so proud of Marley's **accomplishments** that a holiday was established on his birthday February 6 after he died in 1981.

Bob Marley followed the Rastafari religion. Rastafarians wear their hair in a style called **dreadlocks**.

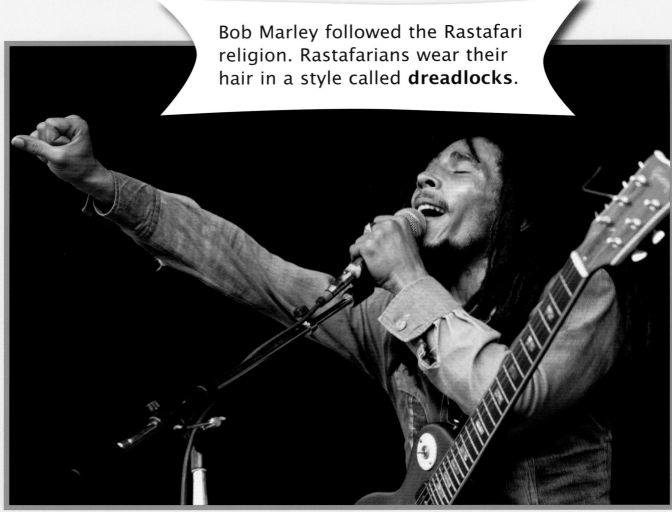

The Bob Marley Birthday Bash annual concert takes place in Montego Bay in Jamaica. Thousands of Jamaicans and tourists attend. People living in Kingston, Jamaica's capital city, enjoy a week-long festival that is all about Marley. Concerts, a fashion show, movies, and exhibitions highlight Bob Marley's contribution to the music industry and the culture of Jamaica. Some Jamaican radio stations play Bob Marley songs all day long on February 6!

Bacchanal Jamaica

Carnival is a happy celebration that takes place in many countries all around the world. Jamaica celebrates its own kind of Carnival called Bacchanal Jamaica. Bacchanal is a word that means a wild and crazy party! Although Carnival in Jamaica is celebrated around Easter time, it is not celebrated for religious reasons. It's just an excuse to throw a big party!

Jamaica's Bacchanal was based on Carnival in the neighboring island nation of Trinidad.

Did You Know?
Carnival in other countries is a very old celebration that began hundreds of years ago. But Jamaica's Bacchanal celebrations only began in 1990!

Bacchanal Jamaica features a parade of colorful floats, live music, and dancers in spectacular costumes. Teams, called Mas Camps, gather together months before the parade, or "road march." Every year, a different theme or idea is chosen for Bacchanal Jamaica and teams compete to make the best float.

17

Easter

Most Jamaicans follow the Christian religion. Easter is a religious holiday observed by Christians around the world. The holiday falls anytime between late March and late April. Easter is a time when Christians remember Jesus Christ's death on Good Friday and his return to life on Easter Sunday.

Christians honor Jesus Christ by attending church services at Easter.

Did You Know?
A Jamaican tradition at Easter is eating a sweet bun with cheese. These Easter buns are filled with raisins, cinnamon and other dried fruit.

A Caribbean Easter legend says that Christ's cross was made from a physic nut tree. If you cut a physic nut tree on Good Friday, the legend says the tree sap will be red like Christ's blood.

On the Thursday night before Good Friday, a custom in Jamaica is to leave an egg white in water. The shape it has formed by the next morning tells you what will happen to you in the future. Does it look like a plane? Maybe you'll take a trip! Flying kites at Easter is another popular activity. An international kite festival is held every year at Easter time in Ocho Rios. The kites are made out of local materials such as bamboo.

Labor Day

Labor Day is a national holiday in Jamaica on May 23. On this day, Jamaicans remember a hero named Samuel Sharpe. Born a slave, Sharpe became a preacher and led other Jamaican slaves in a protest that led to **rebellion**. The slaves won their freedom in 1831. Sharpe, however, was captured and put to death on May 23, 1832.

This sculpture represents preachers Sam Sharpe and Paul Bogle encouraging slaves to refuse to work.

Groups like Le Antonio's Foundation gather to clean up or fix public areas.

Since it began in 1972, Labor Day in Jamaica has been a time when people volunteer, or offer, to take part in community projects. Groups gather to clean up or fix public areas such as roads, schools, and churches. Some plant trees or shrubs on Labor Day. In 1989, Jamaica's government decided to come up with a yearly theme for volunteers, such as helping the environment and respecting the elderly.

Did You Know?
Before 1961, Jamaicans celebrated May 24 as Empire Day to honor the birthday of Great Britain's Queen Victoria. When the holiday was dropped, a new Labor Day holiday was created for May 23—the date of Samuel Sharpe's execution.

Emancipation Day

Emancipation Day is a national holiday in Jamaica on August 1. Emancipation means to be set free from someone else's control. On this day in 1838, a law was passed in Great Britain that gave Jamaica's 311,000 African slaves their freedom. Jamaicans also call this day "Full Free," since only some were freed four years earlier, and "Augus' Mawnin," which is patois for "August morning."

This photo was taken in Jamaica on Emancipation Day to mark the historic occasion

On the night before, people gather at churches or town halls to drum, ring church bells, and celebrate until the morning of Emancipation Day. Some gather to listen to an official reading of the important proclamation to remember their ancestors' struggle.

Did You Know?
Queen Victoria signed the Emancipation Proclamation in 1834. It gave all slaves under the age of six their freedom right away. All remaining slaves were set free four years later on August 1, 1838.

Independence Day

Independence Day is a national holiday in Jamaica that is celebrated on August 6. Jamaica became an **independent** country on this date in 1962. Before then, Jamaica was a **colony** ruled by Great Britain. The first Jamaica Festival was held in 1963 to celebrate Independence Day and Jamaican culture. Each year, a competition is held to choose the Festival Song. The winner gets one million dollars!

Did You Know?
In 1962, the country of Jamaica lowered Great Britain's flag for the last time and proudly raised their own for the first time: green for the land, gold for the sun, and black for strength to overcome hardship.

During Jamaica Festival, people take part in a number of arts competitions such as painting, dancing, cooking, costume making, and songwriting. The Independence Day parade in Kingston has floats, dancers in costumes, and famous Jamaicans. The parade leads to the National Stadium in Kingston where a Grand Gala, or party, is held to show off the best of Jamaica!

National Heroes Day

National Heroes Day falls on the third Monday in October. Jamaica honors a group of seven national heroes from its history. Maroon slaves Granny Nanny and Samuel Sharpe, and preacher Paul Bogle fought side by side with Jamaica's slaves for freedom. **Activists** Marcus Garvey and George William Gordon were Jamaican heroes that fought against injustice. Lawyer Norman Manley negotiated Jamaica's independence from Great Britain.

Manley's (far right) cousin Alexander Bustamante (far left) became the first prime minister after independence.

South African President Thabo Mbeki places flowers at the statue of Jamaican National Hero Marcus Garvey at National Heroes Park.

Did You Know?
Granny Nanny is the only female of Jamaica's seven national heroes. She led her people in the Maroon War from 1720 to 1739.

Wreaths are laid at the monuments of each hero at National Heroes Park in Kingston. Awards are given to citizens who have worked to make Jamaica a better country. National Heroes Day ends a week-long cultural festival known as **Heritage** Week.

Christmas

Christmas is celebrated on December 25. Like other Christians around the world, Christians in Jamaica go to church on Christmas Eve or Christmas morning to celebrate the birth of Jesus Christ. A traditional drink of the season is a spiced drink called sorrel. Sorrel is a red flowering plant found in Jamaica. The leaves are boiled in water. Ginger and sugar are added.

Jamaicans inherited many Christmas traditions from the British. In Jamaica, they put a spin on traditional English Christmas pudding by soaking it in rum.

The Grand Market is an old Christmas Eve tradition that is still celebrated in some places. Streets are closed off so that no vehicles can get through. Shops are decorated with twinkling lights. Shopping, eating, drinking, and street dances go on until the early hours the next morning!

Large cities such as Kingston and Montego Bay hold tree-lighting ceremonies. Large decorated trees light up Christmas concerts, fashion shows, and Grand Markets.

Did You Know?
Jamaicans sing "We Wish You an Irie Christmas" with a reggae beat. *Irie* in Jamaican patois means "excellent" or "great."

Boxing Day

Boxing Day falls on the day after Christmas—December 26. It is a public holiday in Jamaica. It is sometimes called Family Day, and families and friends get together to visit, go to the beach, or share a meal. The British brought the Boxing Day tradition to Jamaica along with a favorite activity on this day—musical theater, which they call pantomime. Actors sing and dance and tell folktales. Jamaicans have added their own culture to the pantomime by telling their own folktales and adding island music and *Jonkonnu* dancing.

Did You Know?
A popular Jamaican pantomime character is Anansi, the spider man. Anansi is an old African folktale. The story has been handed down by Africans who were brought to Jamaica hundreds of years ago.

Pitchy-Patchy is a popular Jonkonnu character covered in strips of cloth.

Jonkonnu, sometimes called John Canoe, is a colorful parade of people in costumes and masks. Slaves began the tradition hundreds of years ago around Christmas, when they got a few days rest from work. Back then, slaves dressed up and paraded up and down roads. Today, the tradition is still celebrated by some Jamaicans on Boxing Day. However, traditional Jonkonnu characters such as Pitchy-Patchy and Cow Head show up at most cultural celebrations in Jamaica.

Glossary

abolish To get rid of

accomplishment Something done or achieved

activist Someone who campaigns for some type of social change

alcohol A strong beverage that can make people drunk

ancestry The line of people from whom a person is descended

Christian Someone who follows the teachings of Jesus Christ, whom they believe to be the Son of God

colony A country ruled by a distant country

dancehall A style of music that uses rap and a heavy beat

folktale A story passed orally from generation to generation

heritage Something passed down to others, such as a country's history

Independent Not ruled by others

jerk A spicy and sweet seasoning for grilled meats

lunar calendar A calendar based on cycles of the Moon

lyrics The words of a song

rebellion An act resistance

reggae Music style from Jamaica, combining native, rock, and soul

spirituality Being concerned with religion or religious matters

plantation A large estate on which crops, such as coffee, are grown

tropical Hot and humid

vegetarian Something that does not contain meat

Index